D1307774

Special thanks to my family and friends
for always believing in me.

Why do we celebrate Holi

ISBN-10: 1795312157
ISBN-13: 978-1795312158

This book belongs to:

_____

Pronunciation Guide

Holi : h – oh – lee
Puja: p oo – j ah
Mantra: mahn – truh
Holika: h-oh-l-ee-k-ah
Dahan: duh – a – n
Hiranyakashyap: hee – ran – yuh – kash – yuh – p
Prahlad: pruh – lad
Vishnu: Vee – sh – noo
Krishna: kree – sh – nah
Malpoa: mal – poh – ah
Gujjiya: goo – jji – yah

Meanings

Holi : Hindu spring festival
Puja: the act of worship
Mantra: a word or a phrase repeated as a prayer
Dahan: an act of burning something

Come, let's celebrate

HOLI

Written and illustrated by
Anitha Rathod

Red from hibiscus,
pink from rose,
green from the leaves and
yellow from beautiful
marigold.

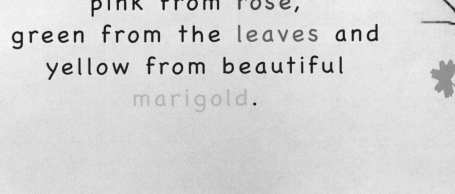

My garden looks as colorful and bright as the
colors of Holi.

The night before Holi, everyone gathered for the bonfire.

At first, I thought we are going to roast marshmallows. But, this bonfire was different.

My Grandma knows best.

So, I ask her curiously, "What is happening, Grandma?"

She smiled and said, "Oh dear, this is called Holika dahan. It is an important ritual of the Holi festival."

She said, "Let me tell you the story behind Holi."

My friends and I sat down to listen to my Grandma. Story-telling time with her is more fun than watching my favourite TV show.

Once, there lived an
evil and powerful king,
Hiranyakashyap.

He considered himself a God and ordered everyone to worship him and only him.

Hiranyakashyap's son, Prahlad, refused to obey his father.

He worshipped Lord Vishnu.

This made the King angry, and he decided to punish Prahlad.

Hiranyakashyap ordered his men to throw Prahlad from the highest point of the fort. Prahlad fell to the ground, unhurt.

The King then ordered Prahlad to be stamped by a giant elephant. But this time again, Prahlad escaped unhurt.

Lord Vishnu saved him from all dangers.

Hiranyakashyap's sister Holika had a shawl that prevented the fire from harming her.

So the king thought Holika could help him punish Prahlad. He asked Holika to take Prahlad in her lap and sit on a pyre.

As the flames grew, the shawl flew from Holika and covered Prahlad. He came out unharmed, and Holika burnt.

Since then, Holi is celebrated with the burning of pyre. This is called Holika dahan. It signifies the victory of good over evil.

Lord Krishna, with his playful nature, celebrated Holi with colors.

Hence, the tradition of playing with colors became part of Holi festival.

Grandma said, "Tomorrow we will celebrate Holi with colors."

The next morning, people splashed colors on each other with water-guns and color powders.

Some were covered in colors from head-to-toe. Some were fully drenched in colored water.

We all started to look like mini rainbows.

Soon, I saw three men arriving with drums. People sang folk songs and danced.

We all danced like no one was watching. Now I know why Holi is called the fun festival.

That evening, we visited our relatives and friends to exchange gifts. We enjoyed the traditional Indian delicacies – Malpoas and Guijiyas, together.

And that's how I celebrated HOLI.

Colorful facts about HOLI

Lathmar Holi,
celebrated in the state
of Uttar Pradesh, is a
tradition where women
hit men with canes
playfully and chase
them away during the
celebration.
Men come prepared
with shields.

In the state of Kerala, Holi is celebrated with
turmeric and other natural colors.

Grand processions are
carried out in many
parts of India.
Music and dance are an
essential part of the
Holi celebration.

Holi is a festival that is meant to bring the
community together and celebrate the spirit of
brotherhood.

Holi is celebrated all over India in many unique
and exciting ways. Every region might have
different traditions and customs, but it unites
everyone with the colors of Love.

Author

This book is a part of the festival series. Every festival comes with a legend and history of its own. I believe through these books, we can learn to stay connected to our roots and traditions.

I hope lots of kids enjoy reading this book and appreciate the true spirit of the Holi festival.

www.anitharathod.com

If you liked this book, I would be really greateful if you could leave a review on Amazon.

HAPPY HOLI